Anchored
to *Hope*

15-Minute Devotions to Activate Your Faith

by

JOY W. YANCY

Anchored to Hope: 15-Minute Devotions to Activate Your Faith
Published by Watersprings Publishing,
a division of Watersprings Media House, LLC.
P.O. Box 1284 Olive Branch, MS 38654
www.waterspringspublishing.com
Contact publisher for bulk orders and permission requests.

Copyright © 2022 Joy W. Yancy. All rights reserved.

No part of this publication may be reproduced, distributed, or transmitted in any form or by any means, including photocopying, recording, or other electronic or mechanical methods, without the prior written permission of the publisher, except in the case of brief quotations embodied in critical reviews and certain other noncommercial uses permitted by copyright law.

Scripture quotations are taken from the New Revised Standard Version Bible, except where noted. Copyright © 1989 the Division of Christian Education of the National Council of the Churches of Christ in the United States of America. Used by permission. All rights reserved.

Scripture quotations, NIV, are taken from the Holy Bible, New International Version®. NIV® Copyright 1973, 1978, 1984 by International Bible Society. Used by permission of Zondervan. All rights reserved.

Scripture quotations marked (NLT) are taken from the Holy Bible, New Living Translation, copyright © 1996. Used by permission of Tyndale House Publishers, Inc., Wheaton, IL 60189 USA. All rights reserved.

Scripture quotations marked "NKJV" are taken from the New King James Version. Copyright © 1982 by Thomas Nelson, Inc. Used by permission. All rights reserved.

Printed in the United States of America.

ISBN-13: 978-1-948877-97-8

*To my husband David Yancy II
for gently pushing me out of my comfort zone.*

Table of Contents

Introduction 1
It's Not About Me 2
The First Day 4
Waiting with Patience 6
Faith Defined 8
Stretch Up for Better! 10
Keep It Simple 12
Surely, It Will Come 14
Accept the Challenge 16
Be Prepared 18
Number Your Blessings 20
God Sees and Knows, So Be Yourself 22
Do You Hear the Rain? 24
Made Well 26
Be A Witness 28
Faith Fight 30
The Strength of Christ 32
Hopeful Character 34
Wait With a Courageous Heart 36
Open Your Ears 38
Don't Grow Weary 40
Trust In God 42
Finish the Race 44

Faith Walk	46
Prepare for Peace	48
Look Up in Faith	50
Hold Fast	52
Shield of Hope	54
Steadfast Hope	56
Appreciate the Ordinary	58
Live a Joy-filled Life	60
New Birth	62
Praise Again	64
Saving Grace	66
Grounded in Love	68
Fulfilling Love	70
Count on God	72
Keep Your Hope Up	74
Right Restoration	76
My Portion	78
Justice Rising	80
Gracious Giving	82
A Song of Thanks	84
Trust in the Eternal Rock	86
Go Do the Impossible	88
In God's Hand	90
Follow the Level Path	92
Power and Strength	94
Inner Strength	96
Hope for My Soul	98
Glory and Hope!	100
Conquering Faith	102
Hope Filled	104
Heirs By Grace	106
Hope in the Lord	108
Speak Hope	110
About the Author	112

Introduction

Have you lost hope of fulfilling your dreams? Are you at a point where you want to quit? Are you anchored to your comfort zone but desire something different? As we grow older and life presents unexpected challenges, it may be easy to say "not now" or "not ever" to the dreams we were passionate about before the spouse, the children, and the gray hair came along. Instead, we have settled for the unfulfilling job because it pays the household bills, college tuition, and eldercare.

The Covid-19 pandemic has not made things better. While some people took advantage of sheltering in place and started a business, wrote a book, or drew closer to God, many lost hope. Being quarantined away from family, friends, co-workers, and church members left many depressed and ready to give up. *Anchored to Hope: 15-Minute Devotions to Activate Your Faith* encourages you to keep your hope up and reignite your dreams. The devotions inspire you to detach from your comfort zone and launch into the deep to manifest your dreams.

Each devotion in *Anchored to Hope is titled and anchored with a key scripture followed by a faith-activating song, prayer, and space for reflection.* The devotional is designed for you to select a topic each day that meets your spiritual need. Be inspired to meet your goals as you spend 15-minutes in the presence of God. For example, read and meditate on the scripture and devotion for five minutes, allow the song to guide you in prayer for five minutes, and journal your reflections for five minutes.

As *you meditate, sing, and pray, may you be encouraged to launch into the deep and fulfill your God-given dreams as you* drop your anchor at the point of your destiny.

It's Not About Me

It is my eager expectation and hope that I will not be put to shame in any way, but that by my speaking with all boldness, Christ will be exalted now as always in my body, whether by life or by death.
Philippians 1:20

"I quit!" "I am throwing in the towel!" While I did not literally say those words, it is what I did – temporarily, at least. The level of change I navigated this past year has been overwhelming. I, like many, adjusted to working from home during a global pandemic. However, I also adjusted to being newly married, embracing new family dynamics, serving as a pastor, and recovering from rotator cuff surgery during a pandemic. There were so many moving pieces, I could not juggle them all, so I just stopped trying and let the pieces fall.

Well, physical therapy is not something you can just let fall if you want to regain full range of motion and return to normal physical activity. To get better, you must press past your feelings and endure the pain. Of course, the therapists say it is not supposed to be painful. As you do the suggested exercise, move until you feel a "good stretch," then hold for 3 - 10 seconds, depending on the exercise, and release. Well, I can tell you from experience, doing three sets of 10 or two sets of 15 of multiple exercises for 45 minutes or more can be painful. However, if you are disciplined to do the work both at physical therapy and at home, it will get better. Eventually, the pain will subside, and range of motion will be gained.

Remember, it is not about you. If you want to be the best God is calling you to be, you must stretch beyond normal limits. If you want to be physically fit to advance the kingdom, you must be disciplined to exercise the body and eat healthily. This is not only true of the physical body but our spiritual body as well. If we want to speak boldly on Christ's behalf, we must stay in God's Word. Listening to the preacher on Sunday or whenever is convenient virtually is not enough. We must study to show ourselves approved. We must sit and listen so we can hear specifically what God is saying to us. Then, when you have clarity, act knowing it is not about you but God's glory, so press toward the prize, not for your benefit but so Christ will be magnified.

FAITH-ACTIVATING SONG

Listen to "Testimony" by Marvin Sapp

PRAYER: Creator God, give me the courage to not give up when the going gets tough. Amen.

REFLECTION:

The First Day

> *"For I know the plans I have for you,"*
> *declares the Lord, "plans to prosper you*
> *and not to harm you, plans to give you*
> *hope and a future."*
> **Jeremiah 29:11 NIV**

Today is a fresh start. It is the first day of the year - calendar or fiscal. It is your birthday or anniversary. Today is the first day of school. It may be the first day of a new job or the last day of work where you have been for twenty-five or more years. Tomorrow will be your first day of retirement.

The original title of this devotional was fifty-two faith exercises and began as a journey for fifty-two weeks of the year. My flesh wanted the devotional to come out at the end of the calendar year so people could purchase and be ready to kick-off the new calendar year. I now know that anytime, any day, any moment, any season can be a fresh start. Doing things based on a chronological calendar year is typical. It is the norm, but God is anything but normal. We can make our plans, but the Lord determines our steps (Proverbs 16:9).

As we spend time with God in prayer and listen to what He has for us to do, God will reveal His plans for us. They are plans not to harm us but to give us hope and a future. So, no matter what day it is, the last day of this or the first day of that, or just being grateful to wake up today, you can be purposeful in pursuing the plan God has for you. Stretch out on God's Word so you can make the most every day for God's glory. Let your light shine as you strive for good success.

FAITH-ACTIVATING SONG

Listen to "Order My Steps in Your Word"
by GMWA Women of Worship

PRAYER: Father God, Creator of heaven and earth. Please order my steps in Your Word. Lead me and guide me along the way that my plan may align with Your plan for my life. Let every day be an opportunity for a fresh start to walk worthy of the calling for which I was called by You. Amen.

REFLECTION:

_____

_____

_____

_____

_____

_____

_____

_____

_____

_____

_____

_____

_____

_____

Waiting with Patience

*For in hope we were saved. Now hope that is seen is not hope.
For who hopes for what is seen? But if we hope for what we do not see,
we wait for it with patience.*
Romans 8:24-25

Waiting, waiting, waiting! Waiting at the doctor's office. Waiting in line at the post office. Waiting in line at the drive-thru for food or financial services. However, there is a difference between waiting as part of our daily routine and waiting for our hopes and dreams to be fulfilled. When we pull up to our favorite fast-food restaurant and see a long line of cars, we have a choice to make. Do we get in line and wait for the food that we probably don't need anyway, or do we head home and eat some already paid for and presumably healthier food?

This is a simple choice within our control to make happen rather quickly. However, when it comes to the things we hope for but cannot see, we have to stretch our vision and wait for it with patience. There are actions steps the Lord calls us to take, but we cannot see all the way down the road. We are called to trust God. While I waited on God for a thing I was hoping for, He provided things for which I was not hoping - like becoming a pastor.

Being a pastor is a major responsibility, but God said be faithful over a few things, and I will put you in charge of many things. Don't waste the talents God has given you. Take the limits off and watch God enlarge your territory. Wait with patience for God's glory to be revealed in your life.

FAITH-ACTIVATING SONG

Listen to "Show Me Your Glory" by Earnest Pugh

PRAYER: Creator God, Thank You for showing me the invisible. Thank You for the patience to wait, to wait for it to come to fruition. Give me the strength to walk in Your will and Your way while I wait. In Jesus' name, Amen.

REFLECTION:

_____

_____

_____

_____

_____

_____

_____

_____

_____

_____

_____

_____

_____

_____

Faith Defined

*Now faith is the assurance of things hoped for,
the conviction of things not seen.*
Hebrews 11:1

The Amplified Bible, Classic Edition puts it this way: Now faith is the assurance (the confirmation, the title deed) of things [we] hope for, being the proof of things [we] do not see and the conviction of their reality [faith perceiving as real fact what is not revealed to the senses]. I like the last part - faith perceiving as real fact what is not revealed to the senses. In the flesh, we may say seeing is believing, or if I don't hear it with my own ears, I will not believe.

Yet, faith in God is when you trust and believe the fulfillment of the promise before it occurs. Then, you can take the promise to the bank and use it as collateral. God honors His Word. Eugene Peter's Message Translation says the fundamental fact of existence is that this trust in God, this faith, is the firm foundation under everything that makes life worth living.

What are you living for? Is your trust in God? Is your faith in the Solid Rock that is higher than us? Keep the faith and see what God will do.

FAITH-ACTIVATING SONG

Listen to hymn "Great is Thy Faithfulness"

PRAYER: Heavenly Father, Let my life be the definition of faith. May I boldly step out on the Solid Rock of Your Word trusting that You will never leave me nor forsake me as You guide me along life's narrow way. Amen.

REFLECTION:

Stretch Up for Better!

*If you direct your heart rightly,
you will stretch out your hands toward him.*
Job 11:13

"Three sets, ten times holding for three to five seconds," the therapist said as they handed me a towel to do wall slides. I was also expected to do the exercise three to four times at home to regain full range of motion. I started out doing table slides, and about six weeks from surgery, I began the wall slides. Talk about painful stretches, yet I pressed through the pain and slid my arm high enough to feel the stretch in my shoulder, hold on a few seconds and release to slide down and REPEAT. You must be disciplined to repeat if you want to get better.

Job was a good man. God acknowledged him as such when he allowed Satan to touch his life. But Job, like all of us, was a human born of a woman, so his life was full of trouble. In spite of, Job trusted God, and God made him better. No, he wasn't perfect, but because of what he endured and how he ultimately responded, God made him better. By the end of the book, Job is both humbled and satisfied, and his fortunes are restored twofold. Job was open to listening. Job stretched beyond his mortal mind to understand the fullness of God. Job, like us, was nothing without God.

As I physically stretched up my arms to get better, I also stretched my eyes to the hills from where my help comes. As I directed my heart rightly, I stretched my hands to God. He lifted me, and I held on, and I'm so much better.

FAITH-ACTIVATING SONG

Listen to hymn "Father, I Stretch My Hand to Thee"

PRAYER: Father, I stretch my hands to Thee, no other help I know; Thank You Lord for not withdrawing Yourself from me. As I stretch up with hand and heart, You draw me in to be better. You draw me in to be more like Your darling Son, Jesus Christ and I am forever grateful. Amen.

REFLECTION:

Keep It Simple

*Then the LORD answered me and said: Write the vision;
make it plain on tablets, so that a runner may read it.*
Habakkuk 2:2

"Make it plain." Sometimes we like to make things too complicated. We feel plain things are simple, unadorned, and even a little boring, so we seek out risk and adventure. We try to impress people by using pretentious, fancy words. We are not content with simple words that the average person is familiar with because we want everyone to know we are college-educated. We don't care if we are understood. As a matter of fact, the goal may be to not be understood, so no one will ask questions (ashamed to show they don't understand), and we get done what we want to get done. But accomplishing your goals to the detriment of others is not what God intended.

Write the vision and make it plain so that a runner may read it and understand it. So, they can read it and understand it while they continue to move forward, while they continue on their way. Life is complicated enough without us adding to it. Don't make people stop unnecessarily because you are complicating matters. We are not all running, walking, moving on level playing fields. Some of us are running up and down hills and valleys. Since we are not all moving on a flat field where we can clearly see what is up ahead, provide a clear vision for guidance so adjustments can be made along the way.

FAITH-ACTIVATING SONG

Listen to "The Vision" by Patrick Love & the A.L. Jinwright Mass Choir

PRAYER: Thank You Lord for doing just what You said in my life. Because I am clear about what You are calling me to do, allow me to help someone else to see the plans You have for their life. Let me be a mentor. Let me encourage someone as they travel on this journey. It is so. Amen.

REFLECTION:

_____

_____

_____

_____

_____

_____

_____

_____

_____

_____

_____

_____

_____

_____

Surely, It Will Come

For there is still a vision for the appointed time; it speaks of the end, and does not lie. If it seems to tarry, wait for it; it will surely come, it will not delay.
Habakkuk 2:3

When I was young, I assumed I would get married. Unlike many, my wedding day was not planned out in my head or in writing. I was not fascinated with wedding dresses, cakes, or rings. I assumed I would get married because my parents were married, and their parents were married. Most of my aunts and uncles were married. Granted, many people in my family also experienced divorce, but the point was they did get married. That is until my generation. I have quite a few cousins who had children out of wedlock. I have two siblings, and for a very long time into our adult lives, none of us were married.

Something I initially took for granted as a given seemed as if it were never going to come to pass. Yet, the vision is for an appointed time. The vision was tarrying, I was waiting, and just around the time that I knew it surely would not come, it came without delay. The one God kept for me until it was time came into my life when needed for the both of us. We both experienced a loss, but God was calling us to move forward. There was more to God's vision than us getting married.

Ecclesiastes 4:9-12 talks about the value of a friend. Operating as a team with God in the midst will bring great things to pass. Wait and see; it will surely come; it will not delay.

FAITH-ACTIVATING SONG

Listen to "Wait on Him" by John P. Kee & the
New Life Community Choir

PRAYER: Creator God, forgive me for assuming and taking Your provision and blessings for granted. You will provide what we need, who we need, exactly when and where we need it. Praise God and Amen!

REFLECTION:

_____
_____
_____
_____
_____
_____
_____
_____
_____
_____
_____
_____
_____
_____
_____
_____

Accept the Challenge

*Commit everything you do to the L*ORD*.*
Trust him, and he will help you.
Psalm 37:5 NLT

A recent Podcast addressed the subject of things not being hard but being challenging. Many may view hard and challenging as synonyms, but it is all about perspective. Usually, we associate hard with difficult things that we do not want to go through, for example, health or financial issues. While we use the word challenging for things, while not easy, we are willing to endure whatever it takes because we focus on the result. Law school or medical school, for instance, may be difficult, but if you desire to become a lawyer or a doctor, then you are up for the challenge. Marriage is hard work, but you are committed to making it work if you want a fruitful relationship. Some may call it semantics, but it is really a mindset.

Certain terms inspire and affirm while other words tear down and deflate. Encourage yourself by speaking life. Whether you are faced with a hard situation or a challenging circumstance, commit it to the Lord. Entrust everything you do to the Lord, and God will help you. As the refrain of "Yield Not to Temptation" goes, "Ask the Savior to help you, comfort, strengthen and keep you; He is willing to aid you, He will carry you through". Trust God to help you through all the situations and circumstances of your life. Whether hard, difficult, and challenging, or easy and carefree, God is able to keep you, so allow God to help you.

FAITH-ACTIVATING SONG

Listen to the Hymn "I Will Trust in the Lord"

PRAYER: God, Please give me the strength to face today's challenges. Give me the strength to commit them to You Lord trusting that You will help me and guide me along the way. In Jesus' name, Amen.

REFLECTION:

_____

_____

_____

_____

_____

_____

_____

_____

_____

_____

_____

_____

_____

_____

_____

_____

Be Prepared

But, as it is written, "What no eye has seen, nor ear heard, nor the human heart conceived, what God has prepared for those who love him"
1 Corinthians 2:9

Preparation is the key to success in life. Life will move forward whether you prepare or not, but you must be intentional if you want to accomplish your goals. If you're going to be ready for future opportunities, you need to take steps now. Years before starting my journey into ordained ministry, I planned to pursue my Ph.D. I enrolled in seminary to obtain a Master of Arts in Religion (MAR) in preparation for doctoral work. My career goal was to teach at a seminary or divinity school. However, while working on my MAR, I accepted my call to preach. I considered switching over to the Master of Divinity program (MDiv) but decided not to because, at the time, I could get ordained as an elder in African Methodist Episcopal (AME) Church with a MAR.

Fast forward a few years, and we are now under a new Bishop who practiced a stricter adherence to the AME Book of Doctrine and Discipline regarding seminary education and ordination. Initially, I was upset, but I chose to return to school and pursue my MDiv. Although I told myself that I was not pastoral and had no intentions to pastor, I was led to prepare myself. I began this journey of itinerant ministry in the AME church, and I was not satisfied with just completing the board of examiners and remaining a deacon. I was led to pursue my ordination as an elder, the highest ordination in the AME church. I did not know, but God knew that less than six months after graduating with my MDiv and one week after getting ordained as an elder that I would be appointed my first charge as pastor. God never ceases to amaze me. We may not see, hear, or conceive, but with God, all things are possible. Prepare yourself to receive the impossible when it comes.

FAITH-ACTIVATING SONG

Listen to Daryl Coley's "He's Preparing Me"

PRAYER: Thank You Lord for the advance preparation. You knew what was up ahead on the journey and You prepared me in advance so I would be ready to handle the situation. Continue to lead me and guide me toward the things I cannot see, I have not heard or conceived. In Your darling Son Jesus' name, amen!

REFLECTION:

_____

_____

_____

_____

_____

_____

_____

_____

_____

_____

_____

_____

_____

_____

Number Your Blessings

Trust in the Lord *with all your heart, and do not rely on your own insight. In all your ways acknowledge him, and he will make straight your paths.*
Proverbs 3:5-6

Numbers have always excited me. I was good at math in school. Well, at least until I reached Advanced Placement (AP) Calculus my senior year of high school. I guess I tried to move too fast. Pre-Calculus was available in preparation for college, but I tried to get in all the AP classes possible, so I could sit for the exams and earn college credit. I was enrolled in AP English and History as well, and not doing well in AP Calculus was a disappointment. My career aspirations shifted from an Electrical Engineer to an Accountant because I was not up for the challenge of the different math classes. Addition and subtraction, along with the debits and credits required for accounting, were more my speed. God was ordering my steps and directing my path even back then.

My husband is a self-employed accountant, and now we are not only partners in ministry, but we are also partners in business. My business background was one of the many things he found attractive when we first met. He encourages me not to hide my skills under a bushel. Although I never sought to be self-employed and practice as a certified public accountant (CPA), after studying for four years and graduating at the top of my class, I was motivated to take the CPA exam and grateful to pass. My husband has my huge certificate hanging on the wall with one of his military honors. God is faithful if we simply trust Him with all of our heart and lean not to our understanding.

FAITH-ACTIVATING SONG

Listen to Kevin Davidson and the Voices' "Count Your Blessings"

PRAYER: Lord, As I look back on disappointing moments in my life, I thank You for turning those situations around for my good. My good days outweigh by bad days. I am grateful as I count my blessings. No matter what math I use, You have provided. If I had ten thousand tongues, I would praise You with every one. Glory, hallelujah to Your precious name. Amen!

REFLECTION:

God Sees and Knows, So Be Yourself

*For human ways are under the eyes of the Lord, and
he examines all their paths.*
Proverbs 5:21

Evangelism used to be an area of struggle for me because I made it more complicated than it was. Considering myself an introvert, I was never bold enough to approach people and talk about Christ. There was the fear of rejection (not necessarily of Christ, but me). If they engaged in dialogue, I did not feel I was up for the debate if they were not ready to be won over. "Taking it to the streets" and knocking on doors was just not me. Actually, it is not a lot of people. But I have since learned that the Great Commission preached about in Matthew 28:19 is not about approaching strangers in pairs to tell them about the Good News and invite them to church.

Over time, with wise human counsel placed in my life by God and studying God's Word for myself, I grew to understand that the Great Commission was about me being my natural self and letting my spiritual light shine. I share my faith naturally, in whatever way I can, with whomever I can, whenever I see an opportunity. I am mindful, willing, and available. I use the tools of social media to reach many that I would never encounter by pounding the pavement or knocking on doors. I demonstrate the Jesus in me through my actions. When asked about the joy I have, I take advantage of the opportunity to share about Jesus Christ. I encourage you to do the same.

FAITH-ACTIVATING SONG

Listen to Whitney Houston's "I Love the Lord"

PRAYER: Lord, give me the courage to tell others about You. I commit to being mindful of You; willing, and available to speak on Your behalf as I go about my daily activities. I love You Lord, so it is not difficult to share the Good News about You. I pray for those who do not know You. I pray their hearts and minds will be open to listen and receive so they can experience Your love and be willing to go tell someone else. In Your name I pray, amen!

REFLECTION:

Do You Hear the Rain?

*Elijah said to Ahab, "Go up, eat and drink;
for there is a sound of rushing rain."*
1 Kings 18:41

When I was younger, Fall was my favorite time of the year. Unlike my younger brother, I enjoyed school. Back-to-school sales signaled that Summer was ending, school would soon start, and shortly after that, Fall would emerge. I enjoyed the cooler weather and bright colors. The leaves changing colors and eventually falling off the trees provided some of the most memorable times from childhood. My maternal grandparents had a huge yard, and we were required to help rake leaves. I remember us taking breaks to run around the yard and jump in piles and throw leaves that were already raked. But of course, my grandmother supervising from the porch soon got us back on task.

We all need wise counsel from time to time to keep us on task. Elijah helped keep Ahab on task. As a prophet, he was able to see things that Ahab could not. Ahab followed his instructions so he could avoid the rain. As I have gotten older, I enjoy Spring as much, if not more, than the Fall. I enjoy the showers that saturate the earth and bring forth blossoms. The newness springing up everywhere motivates me to do all I am called to do before the rushing rain comes. As the sun rises, I feel the presence of the Lord. As the bird chirps, I hear the Lord speaking to me, saying, "Prepare for the journey ahead. Take an umbrella just in case."

FAITH-ACTIVATING SONG

Listen to William McDowell's "Send the Rain"

PRAYER: Father, Thank You for the wisdom and endurance to prepare before the "rushing rain" began to fall. I am grateful for the rain. Rain only matters to those who have seed in the ground. Yes, I have planted, and I look to the Way Maker to send the rain. The harvest is connected to the rain. Praise God for the rain!

REFLECTION:

_____

_____

_____

_____

_____

_____

_____

_____

_____

_____

_____

_____

_____

_____

Made Well

[They] begged Him that they might only touch the hem of His garment. And as many as touched it were made perfectly well.
Matthew 14:36 NKJV

Often life places us at a point where we need the Lord's touch. We need healing, peace, and joy. All we seek is for the Lord to reach from heaven and give us a touch to make everything alright. But there are seasons when the Lord is calling us to press our way and touch the hem of His garment. Faith is required to reach out and touch, believing that God will make all things well. Amazing faith is exhibited in believing that a touch of the hem alone is enough to be made perfectly well.

Several years ago, I experienced a life-changing moment with my mental health. I was at a point of despair and unsure how to come out of the muck and mire. For several years I was going through the motions of life, doing just enough to get by. But I was getting by. I was pressing my way and thanking God for keeping me as I strove to reestablish normalcy in my life. It reminded me of the story of the woman with the issue of blood in Matthew 9:20-22. She did everything she knew to do, and when the opportunity came, she pressed and touched the hem of Jesus' garment. The extra effort makes a difference. Despite the pain and despair, the effort exerted to reach the hem of his garment allowed me to be made whole.

FAITH-ACTIVATING SONG

Listen to Vicki Yohe's "Deliverance Is Available"

PRAYER: Jehovah Rapha, You are a Healer. No matter what I need, physical, mental, or emotional, You are able. Despite what I am going through, I can stretch beyond my limits and experience the difference You make in my life. By Your bruises, I am healed, and I am grateful to be made whole. Amen.

REFLECTION:

Be A Witness

Therefore, since we are surrounded by so great a cloud of witnesses, let us also lay aside every weight and the sin that clings so closely, and let us run with perseverance the race that is set before us.
Hebrews 12:1

On Wednesday, January 20, 2021, we witnessed something never before seen in the history of the United States of America. Kamala Devi Harris took the oath of office as the first female vice-president, the highest-ranking female elected official in US history, the first African American, and the first Asian-American. Vice-President Harris represents excellence. She has received numerous awards and honors because of her track record in her educational and political career. While the majority of us will not excel to the level of becoming Vice-President of the United States, God has an assignment for us, and we are to look to Jesus as our example.

Since we are surrounded by so great a cloud of witnesses, let us also lay aside every weight and the sin that clings so closely and let us run with perseverance the race that is set before us. Yes, run the race set before you. You cannot run anyone's race but your own. Jesus' race was to endure the cross. What is your race? Is it a sprint, a relay, or a marathon? Whatever God has called you to do, run it at your pace so you can make it across the finish line and hear God say, "Well done!"

FAITH-ACTIVATING SONG

Listen to hymn "My Faith Looks Up to Thee"

PRAYER: Heavenly Father, as I reflect on those who have gone before me, I am encouraged to persevere. Continue to give me the strength to walk worthy so I can be a living example in the present and a part of the cloud of witnesses in the future. Amen.

REFLECTION:

Faith Fight

*Fight the good fight of the faith; take hold of the eternal life,
to which you were called and for which you made the good confession
in the presence of many witnesses.*
1 Timothy 6:12

Caregiving is a new phenomenon for me. I have three aging parents whom I help care for from a distance. They fight the good fight of faith as they endure doctor's visits, hospitals stays, and physical therapy. Yet, they stay encouraged as they trust God and know that He is making a way. Even though it is our time as children to care for our parents, they don't want to be a burden, and they want to maintain their independence. They are not necessarily ready to take hold of eternal life.

My mother-in-law is ninety. She owned a flower shop, and it took much persuasion from all five of her children to officially close her business. And even after her business was legally dissolved, she continued to make floral arrangements as a hobby. People know her skills, and they call her to provide flowers and arrangements for funerals and other events. As a matter of fact, she provided the flowers for our wedding.

The compliments received on my bouquet were astounding. She made a smaller bouquet for my matron of honor and matching boutonnieres for the men. Despite her age, she made no excuses. It was an honor and a pleasure for her to do the flowers for her son's wedding; a joyous gift to us. However, she is now coming to accept her physical limitations and may retire "for real" from the flower-making business. She has fought the good fight of faith, but now it is time for the next generation to take the lead in the family business.

FAITH-ACTIVATING SONG

Listen to hymn "Tis So Sweet to Trust in Jesus"

PRAYER: Father, I take You at Your word. You determine when the fight on earth is done. You are not calling me to quit, but to fight the good fight of faith. I trust Your guidance on when to pass the baton to the next generation. Until you call me home, I will cheer others on and encourage them to fight the good fight of faith. Amen.

REFLECTION:

_____

_____

_____

_____

_____

_____

_____

_____

_____

_____

_____

_____

_____

_____

The Strength of Christ

I can do all this through him who gives me strength.
Philippians 4:13 NIV

I know the importance of discipline to accomplish certain projects. As a task-oriented person, I have my activities planned out on my calendar to ensure my goals are accomplished on time. However, some days it is tough to get started. You set your alarm to get up earlier than usual to complete the tasks for the day, but your heart is just not into it. While you manage to get up, you find yourself procrastinating, doing everything but the assignment, which led you to get up early in the first place.

On days like these, my true desire is to return to bed and sleep until my usual wake-up time, but I don't. Instead, I think about my purpose. I remind myself of my end goal. I reflect on assignments that I have completed in the past and encourage myself by saying, "If I did it before, I can do it again." I remind myself of how I accomplished my goals the first time - I remembered that I can do all things through Christ, who gives me strength.

When I focus on Christ's strength in me, it makes the undertaking before me a little bit easier. Honing in on the fact that I am not doing it alone energizes me, and I accomplish even more than I planned to do. Christ uses others to hold me accountable and encourage me that I can do all things through Christ, who gives me strength. Yes, it may be easy to stay in bed, but once you press yourself to put both feet on the floor and get moving, you will be amazed at what you can accomplish with God on your side.

FAITH-ACTIVATING SONG

Listen to William Murphy's "You Are My Strength"

PRAYER: Creator, As I rise this morning, I stretch my arms toward heaven. I thank You for waking me up and praise You in advance for giving me the strength to accomplish Your God-given purpose for the day. Amen.

REFLECTION:

Hopeful Character

And not only that, but we also boast in our sufferings, knowing that suffering produces endurance, and endurance produces character, and character produces hope, and hope does not disappoint us, because God's love has been poured into our hearts through the Holy Spirit that has been given to us.
Romans 5:3-5

"It's hot out here! I'm going inside to the A/C," I shared with my husband as he stood over the grill. Being outside in the heat, especially accompanied by mosquitoes, is not my idea of fun. However, I have not always been opposed to the outdoors. I grew up in the country, and my maternal grandfather was a farmer. He raised tobacco along with chickens and pigs. My brother and I spent a lot of time outdoors in the summer around the pigpen and the chicken coop.

However, I never spent any time in the fields pulling tobacco. As I got older, my preference was to stay indoors curled up with a good book. My early jobs as a teenager were administrative, doing office work. I went to school to obtain an accounting degree so I could work in corporate America. I had no intentions of doing hard labor.

Well, my intentions and the Lords often are not the same. During a challenging time in my life, when I was underemployed in my office job by day, I obtained a manual labor position overnight to have adequate insurance. This was a humbling experience that I endured for almost two years. Endurance produces character, and character produces hope. I'm a living witness that hope does not disappoint because of God's love that has been poured into my heart.

FAITH-ACTIVATING SONG

Listen to hymn "My Hope is Built on Nothing Less"

PRAYER: Lord, Thank You for Your loving-kindness and faithfulness on this journey. As I reflect on the many character-building experiences You have seen me through, my soul cries out "Hallelujah!" Praise God, hope does not disappoint. Amen.

REFLECTION:

Wait With a Courageous Heart

Wait for the Lord*; be strong,
and let your heart take courage; wait for the* Lord*!*
Psalm 27:14

A friend posted on Facebook, "Every day you're given the opportunity to be great. Go ahead and seize the opportunity!" The post reminded me to "let my heart take courage." So often, we operate based on our brain, which makes sense. The brain is where our intellect occurs, and when we make decisions, it is better to use intellect than emotion or instinct. Wise, rational choices tend to work out better for us in the long run than irrational ones. When our emotions get the best of us, we are not waiting on anyone, especially not the Lord. The first thing we feel like doing, we do it without consideration of the consequences.

However, "let my heart take courage" is a balance between operating based on intellect and emotions. The Word says, *"Above all else, guard your heart, for everything you do flows from it" (Proverbs 4:23)*. Our passion comes from the heart, and if we are not careful, we will let our brain talk us out of pursuing our passion. We may experience some apprehension, but if we wait on the Lord, He will give us the courage and the strength to do things we otherwise thought impossible. Your purpose is wrapped up in your passion.

Letting your heart take courage does not mean you are irrational or irresponsible. It means you are being purpose-driven. You are taking a leap of faith to do what God is calling you to do. Seize the opportunity to go with the flow of the heart. Christ will meet you there.

FAITH-ACTIVATING SONG

Listen to Bishop Paul Morton's "Flow to You"

PRAYER: God, thank You for being with me. I take You at Your word when You say You will never leave me nor forsake me. Because of this, I am bold enough to follow my heart and seize the opportunities to be great. I do not seek these opportunities for my glory, but to give You all the glory, all the honor, and all the praise. Amen.

REFLECTION:

Open Your Ears

*So faith comes from what is heard,
and what is heard comes through the word of Christ.*
Romans 10:17

A popular song by Marvin Gaye is titled "I Heard It Through the Grapevine." Part of the song lyrics goes, "people say believe half of what you see and none of what you hear," which is from an Edgar Allen Poe quote. Unfortunately, in today's entertainment and social media-driven society, people believe too much of what they see and hear despite the source's credibility. As a matter of fact, the less credible the source seems, the more the information is believed. Tabloids appear to carry more weight than fact-based news sources.

Well, Jesus is the way, the truth, and the life, and every word spoken by Jesus can be believed. Yet, everyone who heard it did not believe it. The Gospel is truth, but many rejected the Good News. Despite the benefits, they were not convinced that Jesus was the Messiah. Jesus was not a respecter of person but showed the same love to all. This message was not sensational enough; there had to be more.

What more do you need to hear? If the word comes from Christ, that should be enough. Ground your faith in the word of truth, which is Jesus Christ.

FAITH-ACTIVATING SONG

Listen to William Murphy's "It's Working"

PRAYER: Adonai, I am grateful for the truth of Your Word. Ignoring the paparazzi and tabloid reports, I stand in faith on the truth of Your Word. As I open my ear, I hear clearly what You would have me to say and do. I eagerly obey Your instructions knowing they are for my good. Amen.

REFLECTION:

Don't Grow Weary

*So let us not grow weary in doing what is right,
for we will reap at harvest time, if we do not give up.*
Galatians 6:9

As the rain pitter-pattered on the roof, I reached for the snooze button, thinking this was a great day to sleep in. Just a few more minutes, I told myself. I rolled on my side and curled up in a ball, rethinking my day. Cloudy, rainy days have a way of making us rethink our to-do list. The longer you lay in bed, the easier it becomes to shift items from today to tomorrow or later in the week. But when you think about the greater goal, you cannot surrender to the alarm clock. Regardless of the weather outside, the work must go on. Like the USPS, rain, sleet, snow, or chasing dogs, the mail must be delivered. In a season of political and civil unrest, we cannot grow weary in doing what is right.

Resting on our laurels is not an option. We can take a break, a quick pause to celebrate milestones but there is always work to be done. If we grow weary in doing what is right, the advances that have been made will be wiped away. We must keep pressing for the advancement of everyone, particularly those who cannot fight for themselves. If we endure and do not give up, we will reap at harvest time. Harvest time may not come in our generation, but for the sake of the future generation, we must keep pressing, even in the rain.

FAITH-ACTIVATING SONG

Listen to hymn, "I'm on the Battlefield for My Lord"

PRAYER: Lord, I appreciate You giving me the courage to stay on the battlefield. No matter what comes, I will not become weary in doing well. I may have to rest sometimes, but after a period of renewal and restoration, I keep pressing. Even if I must put up an umbrella, I will keep pressing in the rain. For the sake of Your Kingdom and the generations coming behind me I push forward. Amen.

REFLECTION:

Trust In God

*And again, I will put my trust in him. And again,
"Here am I and the children whom God has given me."*
Hebrews 2:13

"Here am I and the children whom God has given me." I am a newlywed. I am married to a man who has three adult children and two grandchildren. I don't have any biological children, but by marriage, I'm now the mother of three and the grandmother of two. Motherhood has somewhat been a challenge because my husband was a widower. His children spent all of their lives knowing their mother, so it was a challenge to have someone new come into their father's life and for us to get married. We are all starting to warm up to our new relationships. I am not only a mother, but I have also become an auntie, sister-in-law, and daughter-in-law.

The Word says to put my trust in God, and so in every situation and relationship, I am trusting God to be in the midst. I now have four sisters-in-law, a brother-in-law, and a mother-in-law. And of course, my husband has two new brothers-in-law, father-in-law, and mother-in-law. God is calling us to put our trust in Him because relationships are not easy. People have different personalities, but God changes not. He is the same yesterday, today, and forever so, we put our faith and trust in Him, He will carry us through.

FAITH-ACTIVATING SONG

Listen to hymn, "I Trust in God (Wherever I May Be)"

PRAYER: Oh, Wise God, I ask for guidance as I take the first step. Encourage me to contact a relative, by blood or marriage, where relationships are strained. Open my heart and mind to the opportunity to invite them. May their hearts be softened to accept the invitation. We would be nothing without You. Wherever I may be Lord, I strive to trust You more. Amen.

REFLECTION:

Finish the Race

*I have fought the good fight,
I have finished the race, I have kept the faith.*
2 Timothy 4:7

"Run Forrest, run" is a famous quote from the movie Forrest Gump. I don't recall why Forrest was being encouraged to run, but I do recall that his life was filled with challenges. Yet, he viewed life with a sweet perspective. Another well-known quote from Forrest Gump is, "life is like a box of chocolates. You never know what you're gonna get." But even though we never know what we're going to get in life, we are called to run the race. We are called to face the various situations which come our way. Whether they're gooey or solid; whether they're dark or light; whether they're fruity or bitter, we must bite into them and see what they have to offer.

Life is not perfect. Each day is not the same, but the God we serve is the same, and he is calling us to fight the good fight of faith. If we continue to look to the Lord from which comes our help, He will guide and direct us on the path. We may not be able to see down the track. We may run around in circles; we may have to run through a forest, but God will be with us to guide us into His marvelous light. So, trust Him as you fight the good fight of faith.

There have been challenges in my life from my youth into adulthood. Periods of unemployment and underemployment; period periods of sickness, but God has been faithful. So, as I continue to endure the tests, I will keep running the race until I hear the Lord say, "Well done."

FAITH-ACTIVATING SONG

Listen to Hezekiah Walker's "99 1/2"

PRAYER: Father, I am intentional today about standing for a cause of justice. Give me the courage to not give up the fight. With Your help, I will not stop running until the race is won. Amen.

REFLECTION:

Faith Walk

For we walk by faith, not by sight.
2 Corinthians 5:7

"One More Sunny Day" is one of my favorite Gospel tunes. Waking up and taking a brisk walk on a sunny day is one of my favorite things to do. I remember when my dog and I used to get up every day and go for a walk. As we traveled the neighborhood, walking up and down the street, he was sniffing, using his sense of smell to guide his way. Of course, my eyes were wide open, watching for other people and pets. As we crossed blocks, I looked both ways for cars and bikes. I'm looking around to see what I can see. I'm looking at the trees and up at the sky, reflecting on what is beyond the clouds as they move by. It is a blessing to be able to see and enjoy nature. However, we're not able to see everything that's in front of us. We're not able to look around and catch everything that's coming in life.

However, God calls us to walk by faith and not by sight. As we speak to the Lord and give Him our earnest prayers, we are to trust God to direct us in the way that He would have us to go. Walking by faith and not by sight doesn't mean that you don't take responsibility or make plans. It simply means that we yield our plans to God's plans. We trust Him even when we can't see Him. We trust the path God provides because we know that God is guiding our steps.

FAITH-ACTIVATING SONG

Listen to Hymn "We've Come this Far by Faith"

PRAYER: Lord, As I walk today, may I trust You with all of my heart. Guide me to not lean on my own understanding, but walk by faith as I keep my hope in You. Amen.

REFLECTION:

Prepare for Peace

Do not worry about anything, but in everything by prayer and supplication with thanksgiving let your requests be made known to God. And the peace of God, which surpasses all understanding, will guard your hearts and your minds in Christ Jesus.
Philippians 4:6-7

Deadlines, deadlines, deadlines! We all face them. I have writing deadlines, work deadlines, and church deadlines. Every Sunday, there's a sermon to prepare. Every week there are work projects and personal projects. Deadlines can be stressful, especially when there are consequences for not meeting them. We are in the middle of tax season, and there are penalties for filing late even if you request an extension. Missing business deadlines can result in losing clients. Submitting homework late can impact your grade. However, even with the best planning, we sometimes cannot meet deadlines because of events beyond our control.

Unanticipated events occur related to technology or the weather, for example, that keep activities or events from happening as planned. Have you almost been done with a paper, and it "disappeared" without a means to recover, and you had to start from scratch at the ninth hour? Talk about frustration and stress. But God! All we can do is trust God as we move forward, doing what we know best to do and trust God to do the rest. The word says, "Do not worry about anything but in everything by prayer and supplication with thanksgiving let your requests be made known to God."

When we make our requests known daily as we wake up in the morning, God will guide us on how to spend our day. He will guide us so we can meet those deadlines that are crucial and teach us to defer those things that can wait. The Lord, our Shepherd, will guide us. Sometimes God opens doors where deadlines that previously appeared to be set in stone now allow for some flexibility. We can get an extension. We call that grace.

A God who offers grace also will give us peace that surpasses all understanding. He will guard our hearts and our minds in Christ Jesus, and all we can do is say, "Thank You, Lord!"

FAITH-ACTIVATING SONG

Listen to "Pray" by CeCe Winans

PRAYER: Lord, Thank You for being a gracious God. Help me meet my deadlines today. Give me peace as I step back and put my schedule in perspective. As I surrender my calendar to You Lord, I experience peace that surpasses all understanding. Amen.

REFLECTION:

Look Up in Faith

*What if some were unfaithful?
Will their faithlessness nullify the faithfulness of God?*
Romans 3:3

After admission into the Annual Conference and completing two years of study in the board of examiners, we were on schedule to receive our ordination as deacons in the African Methodist Episcopal Church. As ordained clergy, we could be called Reverend. While ministry is definitely not about titles, it was a good feeling and sense of accomplishment. However, with the change in episcopal leadership, our journey to ordination was thought to be in jeopardy.

Often in life, our journey is impeded. You plan to do certain things. You've worked hard for so many years, and then it's like the rules change midstream. All the work that you've put in suddenly becomes null and void. While it's not a good feeling, you must stay faithful.

When I started the board of examiners (BOE), for instance, you could obtain ordination as an elder with a Master of Arts in Religion. However, while attending the BOE, the requirements changed to a Master of Divinity (MDiv) degree. Momentarily discouraged, I did not give up. I pursued my MDiv, and three years after completing BOE, I graduated with my MDiv. Shortly thereafter, I was ordained an Elder and received my first appointment as Pastor. God had a purpose for me, and because I pressed forward in faithfulness, I received the reward.

FAITH ACTIVATING SONG

Listen to Hymn "My Faith Looks Up to Thee"

PRAYER: Lord, Hear me when I pray. Forgive me for any sins that I have committed by thought, word, or deed. I am grateful that my momentary unfaithfulness did not impede Your faithfulness to me. Thank You for being the loving Savior Divine. Amen.

REFLECTION:

HOLD FAST

Let us hold fast to the confession of our hope without wavering, for he who has promised is faithful.
Hebrews 10:23

Hold and fast are simple words, and most people know what they mean. Hold is defined as grasp or grip, and fast is defined as swift or quick. However, when used together, the two words take on a whole new meaning. In addition to being an adjective, fast is an adverb meaning "so as to be hard to move; securely." Hold fast means to grasp so tightly that it is hard to let go. When the storms of life are raging, holding fast to the confession of your hope means you are secure in the Lord.

You are firmly anchored in God and God's Word. There is no wavering. Look back over your life and reflect on where the Lord has brought you. What is your story? Don't give up. Think about the times you were at the end of your rope, and God gave you the courage to tie a knot and hold on. If God did it before, the Lord is able to do it again.

Hold unswervingly to the hope you profess, for he who promised is faithful (Hebrews 10:23, NIV). God anchors, and God lifts. God promised to hear us and answer us. God has promised to heal us. God helps and holds us as he provides shade on our right hand. God sustains and saves us time and time again. God is a keeper and a cover. God blocks and builds. God favors and forgives. God pushes us and pulls us to be our best for his glory. Hold fast. Don't let go of your faith so you can tell your story.

FAITH-ACTIVATING SONG

Listen to "Blessed Assurance"

PRAYER: Lord God, I rest assured in Your promises. You have never failed me. I trust and believe You never will. I am standing on Your promises. Amen.

REFLECTION:

Shield of Hope

You are my hiding place and my shield; I hope in your word.
Psalm 119:114

During my "Sacred Sisterhood" session today, one of the members used the term "veil of hope" as she spoke about the 2021 Inauguration. As I prayed to open up the group, I reflected on how the inauguration was peaceful. Everything went off without a hitch. After incidents earlier in the month, many were concerned if that would be the case. But daily, I am reminded that God is indeed in control. God is our hiding place and our shield. God is our veil of hope. God protected the President and Vice-President as they stood to take their oath of office. The Lord protected all of those involved and allowed them to present a united and peaceful front. Later that evening, there was a virtual celebration that a new season had come at last.

    I am thankful for new seasons. They are part of the ebb and flow of life. Some seasons are for hunkering down and doing the work. Some seasons are for praising and celebrating. Some seasons are for resting. The Message translation of the above verse says, "you're my place of quiet retreat; I wait for your Word to renew me." God's *veil of hope* provides a place of quiet retreat. We can engage in a Sabbath moment and allow the presence of God to renew us. Once we are renewed, we return to the season of work. The work is necessary. It is part of the circle of life. On certain parts of the journey, we may work more than play but trust the Rock of our salvation to hide and shield us as we hope in His Holy Word.

FAITH-ACTIVATING SONG

Listen to Hymn "Rock of Ages, Cleft for Me"

PRAYER: Lord God, As I take a moment to pause and look back over my life, I am grateful for the times You have protected me. As many times as I can recall, and many more that I was not even aware of when You kept me in the cleft of Your care. Thank You for being a hiding place and a shield for me and those I love. Amen.

REFLECTION:

Steadfast Hope

We have this hope, a sure and steadfast anchor of the soul, a hope that enters the inner shrine behind the curtain.
Hebrews 6:19

The author of Hebrews reminds us of Abraham's faith in God. God's promises provided a spiritual anchor for Abraham in the Old Testament, and they provide a spiritual anchor for us today. Several years ago, the Lord spoke to me as clearly as he spoke to Abraham when God told him to leave his country and follow God to an undisclosed land where God would make him a great nation and a blessing. In a symbolic gesture of obedience, I ran around the sanctuary at church. Less than two years later, I physically left my role as an associate to assist at another church. The clarity of God's Word gave me the power to trust God to leave my comfort zone of almost eighteen years.

As soon as I moved, God enlarged my territory, and I was appointed to pastor my own church. While anchors are necessary to hold position, when it is time to move and launch into the deep, the anchor is lifted to allow mobility. Whether you are physically moving or standing still, our soul needs to be anchored in the Lord. The Lord will never leave us nor forsake us. As we trust God, He will not let us drift too far or be overcome with the winds or the rain. Through the storms of life, keep your hope in the Lord. Jesus is the anchor for our souls, and He will keep us firm and secure as we journey through this thing called life.

FAITH-ACTIVATING SONG

Listen to "My Soul Is Anchored" by Douglas Miller

PRAYER: Creator God, Thank You for sending Jesus to save me and bring me into relationship with You. When my faith falters and fear and doubt fill my mind, remind me that Jesus is my anchor. That You, that Jesus will hold me secure in His love. Amen.

REFLECTION:

_____

_____

_____

_____

_____

_____

_____

_____

_____

_____

_____

_____

_____

_____

_____

Appreciate the Ordinary

Glory in his holy name;
*let the hearts of those who seek the L*ORD *rejoice.*
1 Chronicles 16:10

The mornings, in my opinion, are the best time to spend with the Lord. While I am a morning person, my husband is not. Well, at least not until recently. One day when I planned to get up at 5:15 a.m. to write, he was wide awake and talking. He brought up the subject of walking, which I enjoy. When I was single, I didn't give a second thought to getting up early (although not quite this early) and going for a walk with my dog Jenks.

Since I have been married, I am hesitant to walk by myself, particularly real early in the morning because I know one, my husband will be concerned, and two, he wants to go with me. However, since he is normally in bed, we usually do not walk until later if we walk at all. So, it was a wonderful occasion when we both got up before the sun to take a three-mile nicely paced walk in our neighborhood.

There was nothing spectacular about the walk or the day other than being a day the Lord made, and we chose to rejoice in it together. As you arise each day, decide to seek the Lord and rejoice. As you glory in His name, choose to appreciate the ordinary.

FAITH-ACTIVATING SONG

Listen to "Glory to the Lamb" by Geoffrey Gold

PRAYER: Creator God, I thank You for the breaking of day. I thank You for the opportunity to seek You while You may be found. Lord, I appreciate every day that You have made. Whether it is morning, noon, or night, I seek You and I choose to rejoice. Amen.

REFLECTION:

Live a Joy-filled Life

*Yet I will rejoice in the LORD;
I will exult in the God of my salvation.*
Habakkuk 3:18

That May was filled with productivity. So many exciting things happened, I deemed the month #MindBlowingMay. We celebrated our wedding anniversary with a beach vacation. After enjoying several days out of town, we returned home to a relaxing holiday weekend. The holiday fell on the last day of the month, and June entered full force with busyness. When Friday came, I almost had no memory of our vacation.

Friday is normally our "date night," and whether we go out or stay home, we always plan some fun. This particular Friday, my hairdresser was not feeling well, and she canceled my early morning appointment. Thankfully I was able to secure an appointment with my previous beautician. However, it was no fun returning to the days of being at the hairdresser on a Friday evening after work. I felt drained that week, and as I looked at my calendar for the rest of the month, I did not see how #JubilantJune would manifest.

Yet, I was reminded to rejoice in the Lord. As I chose to exalt in the God of my salvation, I was able to balance work and play. Date night, for instance, does not always have to be on Friday. We can choose to have fun every day as we live a joy-filled, inspired life. My impulse to have fun is the call of my soul to reclaim my joy, to live an exuberant life full of optimism. As I play, my spirit begins to feel lighter as I laugh and smile. I encourage you to commit to making fun a priority in your life.

FAITH-ACTIVATING SONG

Listen to "Joy" by The Georgia Mass Choir

PRAYER: God, Your Word in James 1:2 says, *"Consider it pure joy, my brothers and sisters, whenever you face trials of many kinds."* No matter what we are facing or how busy we are, remind us Lord to carve out time for fun. You told us that unless we change and become like children, we will never enter the kingdom of heaven. So, guide us to never outgrow our love for having fun. Teach us to live a joy-filled life as we work and play. Amen.

REFLECTION:

New Birth

Blessed be the God and Father of our Lord Jesus Christ! By his great mercy he has given us a new birth into a living hope through the resurrection of Jesus Christ from the dead,
1 Peter 1:3

"Inspire, Create, Repeat" stands out in gold cursive letters on my multi-color journal, the second journal I purchased to plan this devotional. My strategist advised me to keep everything related to the devotional in one place. During my first attempt, I purchased a baby blue journal with pink flowers and birds. "Those who hope in the Lord will renew their strength" (Isaiah 40:31) was in the center. I was inspired to use this journal because one of my favorite scriptures was on the cover and the translation of this verse contained the word hope.

However, I was not motivated to write. I later realized I was attempting to structure the devotional as an anchor for something bigger. I was trying to create an ocean plan when I had not completed the assignment God gave me for the kiddie pool. There is nothing wrong with thinking big and planning for success, but God will not honor your dreams when you do not obey His daily instructions.

God gave me a vision for a four-part devotional series. While there will be other opportunities to write and participate in projects simultaneously while I complete this, my plans to "operate in the ocean" will not fully manifest until I finish this devotional project. I successfully participated in a 21-day writing challenge where I was held accountable to write. However, we will not always be held accountable by other people to complete our assignments.

When you know what God has called you to do, pray for the discipline required to complete your assignment. By God's great mercy, He has given me a new birth into a living hope. I am invigorated to "inspire, create, repeat" until this series is done. Are you struggling to bring YOUR plans to fruition? Think back. Do you have an uncompleted God-given assignment? Get to work in the pond and watch God launch you into the deep.

FAITH-ACTIVATING SONG

Listen to "Deeper" by Marvin Sapp or
"It's A New Season" by Israel and New Breed

PRAYER: Lord, Give me the courage to stay focused on Your plans for my life. As I am faithful over the small things, I trust You to enlarge my territory. I thank You for birthing new ideas within me and I trust You to guide me to know what is mine to complete now, in preparation for what You will have me complete later. It is a new season; it is a new day to launch out and be all that You are calling me to be. Amen.

REFLECTION:

_____

_____

_____

_____

_____

_____

_____

_____

_____

_____

_____

_____

_____

Praise Again

Why are you cast down, O my soul, and why are you disquieted within me? Hope in God; for I shall again praise him, my help.
Psalm 42:5

For a while, I allowed the Covid-19 pandemic to get the best of me. I fell into a slump, leaving my hopes and dreams on the back burner. Yet, as I reminded myself to hope in God, I was no longer cast down. I was no longer distressed about working from home, serving as a virtual pastor, or wearing a mask all the time in public.

    As I listened to "Oh Mighty God" from David Carnes' Journey of Praise CD, I activated my praise and began to fulfill God's plan for my life. As I regrouped and began to complete this devotional, I reflected on how mighty and powerful God has been in my life. God has done and continues to do so much for me and my family. Like many, we have been touched by sickness and loss during this season, but we recognize God is in control, and the Lord is working everything out for our good. There is joy amid sorrow and pain.

    When the pandemic hit, I was single. Less than three months into the tumultuous season, I was married. The global epidemic accelerated our wedding plans. Once we decided to forgo a traditional in-person wedding, we said, "Why wait?" We have since celebrated our first wedding anniversary, and for that, I give God praise. What do you have to praise God for? Lift your voice and tell God thank You. Despite it all, be grateful and offer God the fruit of your lips. If you have experienced a slump, come out by offering God your praise again.

FAITH-ACTIVATING SONG

Listen to Rodnie Bryant and the Christian Community Mass Choir's "We Offer Praise"

PRAYER: Oh Lord how mindful I am of the seasons You have caused to change. Likewise, I am thankful for the hope in each season. Teach me to always return to hopeful praise and remind me of the past glory You have received and the new glory yet to be released. From the rising of the sun until the going down of the same, You are worthy to be praised. Glory, hallelujah, amen!!!

REFLECTION:

_____

_____

_____

_____

_____

_____

_____

_____

_____

_____

_____

_____

_____

Saving Grace

*For by grace you have been saved through faith,
and this is not your own doing; it is the gift of God—*
Ephesians 2:8

As I entered the restaurant and greeted the hostess, I held up my hand and said, "Five." As she looked around, I also looked around and saw one person at my party. She was waving and smiling, inviting me to our table. I started smiling when I saw a bright yellow gift bag. There was a card attached with "Joy" written in orange cursive letters. Orange is one of my favorite colors. I automatically sat down in front of my name, and we talked until others arrived. The third person to arrive immediately dove into her bag of goodies, so we all did. We looked forward to blowing our bubbles and chewing our gum. One person immediately tried out her lip balm. We had so much fun.

The giver called the bags "happies," and gifts tend to make us happy and bring us joy. I vividly recall the joy I felt on my 51st birthday when an engagement ring appeared on the table along with my dessert. While they say diamonds are forever, nothing can compare to the joy of receiving the gift of God's grace. For by grace you have been saved through faith, and this is not your own doing; it is the gift of God (Ephesians 2:8). I appreciate Jesus using other people to spread his love with tangible gifts and acts of kindness. I praise God for the unmerited favor of the greatest gift of all, Jesus Christ.

FAITH-ACTIVATING SONG

Listen to "No Greater Love" or
Hymn "Jesus Loves Me, This I Know"

PRAYER: Jesus thank You for loving me. Thank You for the small ways Your love is conveyed everyday as You use the hands and hearts of Your people. Thank You for Your sacrificial love and the grace that came with it. Nothing I do or don't do will ever separate me from Your love. Hallelujah! Amen.

REFLECTION:

Grounded in Love

*And that Christ may dwell in your hearts through faith,
as you are being rooted and grounded in love.*
Ephesians 3:17

During the pandemic, we could not hang out and fellowship with friends and family like normal. Truth be told, I was not hanging out much before the pandemic. I experienced a lot of change which removed me from my previous circle of friends, and I simply did see them on a regular basis. They say absence makes the heart grow fonder, or it makes the heart forget. I felt forgotten by my friends. Thankfully the Lord brought new friends into my life, but I thought of the tune from my childhood, "make new friends but keep the old; one is silver, and the other is gold."

One day the Lord dropped an old friend in my spirit. I sent her a card in the mail to let her know I was thinking about her, and I scheduled a lunch date for once I was fully vaccinated. The Lord confirmed this reunion because a mutual friend of ours sent us a group text mentioning she saw us at a church service in her dream. When Christ dwells in your heart and you are rooted and grounded in love, despite changing situations, you are intentional about maintaining relationships. I'm glad I reached out to my friend, and I'm grateful that I have a friend in Jesus.

FAITH-ACTIVATING SONG

Listen to "Your Love "by William Murphy or
Hymn "There's Not a Friend"

PRAYER: Creator God, I thank You for relationships with family and friends. More importantly, I am grateful for my relationship with Your Son Jesus Christ. There is not a friend like the lowly Jesus, no not one. I am grateful that Christ dwells in my heart. I give praise for Your unexplainable, unconditional love. Amen.

REFLECTION:

Fulfilling Love

*I pray that you may have the power to comprehend, with all the saints,
what is the breadth and length and height and depth,
and to know the love of Christ that surpasses knowledge,
so that you may be filled with all the fullness of God.*
Ephesians 3:18-19

There was much talk about one of the potential Olympic athletes being disqualified for testing positive for cannabis. I remember there was a time when culture would have been on board with the decision. She broke the rules, so she must suffer the consequences, no exceptions. My generation and personality type both lend themselves to following the rules and not expecting to be rewarded if you break them. However, we are living in a different time. The Millennials and Generation Z have a totally different perspective than the Baby Boomers and Generation X, and they have no problem raising their voices.

As a matter of fact, a millennial NFL player said it's "ridiculous" for her to be left of the US Olympic roster. Well, whether it is ridiculous or not, it is a done deal. But that is not the case with us when it comes to the love of Jesus Christ. We can barely comprehend the breadth, length, height, and depth of the love that Jesus has for us. No matter what we have done, Jesus still loves and wants us to achieve our destiny. Jesus wants us to be filled with the fullness of God, regardless of the mistakes we have made. Now that is love.

FAITH-ACTIVATING SONG

Listen to: "No Greater Love" by Greg Sykes

PRAYER: Lord, thank You for Your abounding love. There is no greater love on earth than the love You showed for me by sacrificing your life. I strive to give You the best that I have in appreciation of Your love. I know I cannot repay You, but I just want to praise You. Amen.

REFLECTION:

_____

_____

_____

_____

_____

_____

_____

_____

_____

_____

_____

_____

_____

_____

Count on God

I wait for the L<small>ORD</small>, *my soul waits, and in his word I hope;*
Psalm 130:5

As summer officially begins, I reminisce on my childhood. We looked forward to being out of school and enjoying our free time. Time did not matter as we got up most days without a care in the world. We spent the day outdoors riding our bikes, chasing chickens, and exploring the greenery near the hog pen at my grandparents' house. We came inside for a cool drink and to get a break from the heat. On special occasions, when my cousins came over, my grandmother and one of her sisters would make homemade ice cream on the back porch. The good old days.

As much as I enjoyed hanging out with my brother and cousins in the summer, some of my most memorable times were spent alone in the screened-in front porch of my grandmother's house. I was surrounded by all of her plants. I would sit on the porch, reading and rocking in the glider chair. I had a view of the road leading away from the country to the city. Sometimes I would think about the future, what my life would look like when I was all grown up and no longer spending my summers surrounded by family.

I was counting on the Lord to keep me. Just as the Lord placed family in my life to guide and keep me while I was young, I was hopeful as I matured and left home, He would continue to provide. I waited expectantly to see what the Lord would do. He has never failed me.

FAITH ACTIVATING SONG

Listen to "Wait On Him "by John P. Kee &
New Life Community Choir

PRAYER: Lord You are dependable. I can count on You to keep Your word. You took care of me when I was younger, and You continue to take care of me as I get older. You not only take care of me, but those in my circle of influence and beyond. As my world has expanded beyond my small hometown, I truly realize how You are everywhere at once, and I continue to hope in Your Word to see me through. Amen.

REFLECTION:

_____

_____

_____

_____

_____

_____

_____

_____

_____

_____

_____

_____

_____

Keep Your Hope Up

Rejoice in our confident hope.
Be patient in trouble, and keep on praying.
Romans 12:12 NLT

When the Covid-19 pandemic hit, I began to work from home. Although I used to go into the office daily and sit at a workspace identified with my name, I also had a laptop. So, when my manager called during my vacation to say I did not need to come back to the office, I was relatively prepared. Of course, who knew we would be out for more than a year. If I had known, I would have gone by the office to pick up a few things before we were restricted from entering the building without authorization.

My virtual office has evolved as I coped during this season. I started at a breakfast table, sitting in a narrow chair with light padding. In time I swapped it out for a larger chair with more padding, but it was still a kitchen chair. There was not much on the walls to guide my day, mentally or spiritually. Eventually (better late than never), with the assistance of my husband, my space was rearranged. The kitchen table and chairs were replaced with a desk chair and a portable workstation. I now have items all around me to guide my productivity and motivate me spiritually.

As I lean back in my desk chair to stretch, I am encouraged by a commissioned acrylic wood painting that reads, *"Rejoice in our confident hope, be patient in trouble and keep on praying."* The background of the scripture is an ocean with the sun rising to offer hope for a new day. No matter what troubles you are facing, you can look up with hope and stretch your arms toward heaven knowing, everything will be alright as you keep on praying.

FAITH-ACTIVATING SONG

Listen to Hymn "When Peace Live a River
(It Is Well with My Soul)"

PRAYER: Creator God, Thank You for the rising sun and the gentle breeze off the ocean. Even when I am not able to get away to experience sandy beaches or quiet streams, You allow me the opportunity to commune with You in my present surroundings. Thank You for a work environment that allows productivity and gives me perfect peace. Amen.

REFLECTION:

_____

_____

_____

_____

_____

_____

_____

_____

_____

_____

_____

_____

_____

Right Restoration

He restores my soul.
He leads me in right paths for his name's sake.
Psalm 23:3

The southern girl that I am, on a hot summer day, I find a cool glass of sweet tea refreshing. Yes, I know water is better for me, but some days sweet tea is simply calling my name. One day I grabbed fast food for lunch (I know, another no, no). Initially, I planned to go somewhere that served salads, a presumably healthier fast-food option. However, the cars were in the street, so I opted for the golden arches because I wanted sweet tea. As the young man took my order, he said, "We don't have any sweet tea at the present moment." Disappointed, I ordered fruit punch as the accompanying drink for a chicken nugget meal.

    God knows exactly what we need, or should I say, what we do not need. This trip out for lunch gave me pause to reflect on the necessity of so many things. I had food options at home. With little preparation, I could have eaten without leaving the house in ninety-three degrees heat. I utilized time and gas to not get what I wanted. If we pause, God will restore our souls. The need for sweet tea and fries will subside. Let God lead you on the right paths for His name's sake.

FAITH-ACTIVATING SONG

Listen to "Lead Me, Guide Me Along the Way"

PRAYER: Way-Maker, thank You for leading and guiding me along. I cannot stray if You lead me, I cannot stray. Let everything I do and say, be to Your glory. Amen.

REFLECTION:

_____
_____
_____
_____
_____
_____
_____
_____
_____
_____
_____
_____
_____
_____
_____
_____
_____

My Portion

"The LORD is my portion," says my soul, "therefore I will hope in him."
The LORD is good to those who wait for him,
to the soul that seeks him.
Lamentations 3:24-25

This scripture adorns the wall of our downstairs half bath. When I am experiencing challenging moments, I often find myself standing in the bathroom meditating over this scripture. "The Lord is my portion" reminds me of "our daily bread" from the Lord's prayer. He provides enough of what I need each day. There is no need to worry when I hope in him. The Lord is good to those who wait for him. Another word for wait is trust. As I trust the Lord and seek him with all my heart, I know that everything will be alright.

    The Hebrew word for portion relates to an interest in the favor and love of God, an inheritance. When we are in the presence of the Lord, our hearts let us know that everything is going to be alright, and that is the best inheritance. We have everything we need to balance our troubles and make up for our losses. Inheritances on earth are empty and perishable; God is an all-sufficient and durable portion. Therefore, I will hope in Him. What about you?

FAITH-ACTIVATING SONG

Listen to "Everything Will Be Alright" by Isaiah Templeton

PRAYER: Lord, You alone are my portion and my cup; You make my lot secure. Thank You for the favor of Your love and favor. Thank You for meeting every need; for providing for my spirit, soul, and body. As You provide for me, guide me to provide for others who are unable to do so for themselves. Let them know that everything will be alright as they seek You. Amen.

REFLECTION:

Justice Rising

Therefore the L<small>ORD</small> waits to be gracious to you; therefore He will rise up to show mercy to you. For the L<small>ORD</small> is a God of justice; blessed are all those who wait for Him.
Isaiah 30:18

2020 proved to be a challenging year. The global pandemic and the resulting impact was the first my generation and those younger than me have experienced. I did not live through the Great Depression or the Civil Rights Movement. I was born the year Dr. Martin Luther King, Jr. was assassinated. By the time I entered the world in November, his death in April was old news. I now reside in the city where his death took place. While his birthday is a national holiday, in the city of Memphis, as much, if not more, is commemorated on the anniversary of his death as the anniversary of his birth.

The rights that Dr. King fought continue to be challenged in the twenty-first century. Social injustice, civil unrest, and political tension covered the landscape in 2020. While things are far from perfect, we are beginning to see change. The conviction in the trial for the murder of George Floyd was unprecedented. We now have a female Vice President of the United States of America who is also African and Asian American. As the people continue to take a stand for what is right, the Lord is standing with us.

Don't give up hope that change will come. The L<small>ORD</small> waits to be gracious to us. God will rise to show mercy to us because the L<small>ORD</small> is a God of justice. Blessed are all those who wait for Him. Look up; justice is rising.

FAITH-ACTIVATING SONG

Listen to "Glory "by Common and John Legend

PRAYER: Lord, I pray that the Church will not be complicit of injustice by being silent, but that it can rise with a prophetic voice that speaks truth to power and advances the values of Your Kingdom. I pray these things in the name of our blessed Redeemer, Jesus Christ. Amen.

REFLECTION:

GRACIOUS GIVING

*A generous person will be enriched,
and one who gives water will get water.*
Proverbs 11:25

Generosity is not just about tangible giving. Being generous with our time and attention is vital, particularly with our parents as we become adults. During a recent trip home, my siblings and I worked together to provide an especially enjoyable time for our parents, especially our mother. No matter how old you get, you are still your parents' children, and they want to spend time with you, even if you are doing nothing in particular. The ministry of presence is a gift, and even though I traveled with my husband and stayed at a hotel, I made sure I spent quality time with my mother, stepdad, and father.

The time together was enriching, and I am glad I followed the wisdom of Solomon that he penned in the book of Proverbs. Its thirty-one chapters call the reader to listen to wisdom and avoid folly. Wisdom - knowing what to do when - comes from honoring God by seeking God's ways. The Lord guides us to honor our parents so it may be well with us and our days on the earth will be long. When we honor God and seek God's ways, we will receive the wisdom we need for all the matters we face in life. Each and every one.

FAITH-ACTIVATING SONG

Listen to "I Give Myself Away" by William McDowell

PRAYER: Lord God, remind me that You are the Source of the wisdom I need. Guide me to give myself away so You can use me. Amen.

REFLECTION:

A Song of Thanks

The Lord is my strength and my shield;
in him my heart trusts; so I am helped, and my heart exults,
and with my song I give thanks to him.
Psalm 28:7

"Thank You, Jesus, thank You, Jesus!" I exclaimed as we turned the corner. Prior to my outburst of thanksgiving, God made the way clear so my husband, after quickly looking left, could safely turn so that we could avoid an accident approaching from the right. Sitting in the passenger seat, I just knew the other driver, who suddenly decided to move left to avoid obstacles they saw ahead, was going to crash into us. I did not utter a word audibly. Many thoughts went through my head, along with a brief prayer of protection. My communication with God enabled my heart and emotions to stay calm.

My connection with the Father gave me peace and kept me quiet until we turned the corner. Once we were safe, I could not hold my peace. As I yelled, "Thank You, Jesus," multiple times, my husband parked the car on the side of the street. The Lord is worthy to be praised, and sometimes you have to stop and give Him thanks. You must stop, and with your voice, with your song, give Him thanks. The Lord helped us as we drove downtown on a Sunday afternoon headed to dinner. The Lord shielded us from being hit. For that, we give Him praise. Reflect on what the Lord has done for you today, then stop for a moment to say thank You.

FAITH-ACTIVATING SONG

Listen to "Thank You Lord"
(*Whatever version you prefer. I like to hear Dr. E. Dewey Smith sing.*)

PRAYER: Creator God, today, with my heart, I give You thanks. You made a way. You brought me out. You've been so good, and I am so grateful. I just want to thank You Lord for keeping me and my family safe. I am grateful for Your protection - from dangers seen and unseen. I appreciate Your guiding wisdom on the roads and protection from traffic accidents. I am overjoyed because You are my strength and my shield. Lord, I trust You. Amen.

REFLECTION:

Trust in the Eternal Rock

Trust in the Lord always,
for the Lord God is the eternal Rock.
Isaiah 26:4 NLT

My Lord is an eternal Rock. When you are frustrated with life and try to move in your own way, God slowly walks you down. He tears down your plans and makes you follow His because they are rock-solid. Early in the editing process of a previous book, I became extremely frustrated. Back then, I stressed out easily, and when notified that the edits were taking longer than estimated, which meant more costs, I was quite upset.

As the accountant in me calculated the new estimated total cost, I quickly realized I had to turn it over to God. My plate was full, and to accomplish the other things on my agenda for the week, I needed to pray and go to sleep. All of the "what ifs" can consume our minds, and if we are not careful, we can worry more than we worship. I chose to trust the truth of God's Word, rested well, and awoke with answered prayer. The Eternal Rock always provides.

FAITH-ACTIVATING SONG

Listen to "Lead Me to the Rock" by Stephen Hurd

PRAYER: Creator God, You are the Rock of my salvation. I am grateful to be able to run to You, my solid foundation. When all other ground is sinking sand, You are my Rock on whom I can trust and depend. I want to run to You. Lead me to You. Amen.

REFLECTION:

Go Do the Impossible

For nothing will be impossible with God.
Luke 1:37

One of my girlfriends posted an image on Facebook from @HappyBlackWoman that said, "Think bigger. Ask yourself: If I could do anything I wanted in my life, what would I do? Then go do that." Wow! Really, is that all it takes? Well, the Word does say that nothing is impossible for God. If what I want lines up with His Word, then there is absolutely no reason I should not be able to "go do that."

We often do not believe the truth of God's Word. We say we have faith, but then we pray wimpy prayers or rationalize why our dreams cannot happen. Decide today to take a chance on God. Think bigger and hand your thoughts over to God. Ephesians 3:20 confirms that the Lord can do exceedingly, abundantly above all that we ask or think. So, whatever we think, God is thinking bigger, and because nothing is impossible for God, how about we "go do that."

FAITH-ACTIVATING SONG

Listen to "Greater" by Tasha Cobbs

PRAYER: Jehovah God, Thank You for opening my eyes to see greater, my ears to hear greater and the motivation and will to go do greater. Greater, not by strength but the power of Christ that works in me. When I seek first Your kingdom and Your righteousness, my plan aligns with Your plans and nothing is impossible for me. I am going to "go do that" in Jesus' name. Amen.

REFLECTION:

In God's Hand

But I trust in you, O Lord; I say, "You are my God."
My times are in your hand; deliver me from the hand of
my enemies and persecutors.
Psalm 31:14-15

Walking across the parking lot, I spotted two of my girlfriends laughing and talking in front of the restaurant with their masks on. Of course, I was mask-less. We were all fully vaccinated, and this was our first time getting together in almost a year and a half. We reminisced that the last time we saw each other in person was at one of their baby showers and her son was now fourteen months. My how time passes when you are quarantined. As we waited to be seated, our other friend showed up "late." She was really late since we were on a waitlist, and there were four tables ahead of us at the last check-in.

Waiting while you are catching up and having fun is much different than waiting on the Lord to deliver you from the hand of your enemy. Over the past year and my lifetime, there have been seasons when I was ready to fast forward past the trials and tribulations. I did not want to experience the bodily pains of physical therapy or the emotional pains of new relationships. The Word, however, reminds me that my time is in God's hands. The seasons of challenge and struggle are preparing me for my destiny. In order to get to, I have to go through. I trust You, Lord, and I'm going to wait. Keep your hope up and wait on the Lord.

FAITH-ACTIVATING SONG

Listen to "Wait" by Nina Allen

PRAYER: Lord God, Help me to wait on You. As I abide in Your Word, I will stand still until You tell me to move. Help me to wait, but also give me the courage to move when You say go. Whether I am standing still or going, my time is in Your hands. Thank You for keeping me in Your care. Amen.

REFLECTION:

_____
_____
_____
_____
_____
_____
_____
_____
_____
_____
_____
_____
_____

Follow the Level Path

Teach me to do your will, for you are my God.
Let your good spirit lead me on a level path.
Psalm 143:10

Summer is the time for rest and relaxation. As businesses slow down, owners and employees alike use their paid time off for vacation. The busyness of work is minimized to make room for fun and enjoyment. Preparation is necessary to "go offline" for a few days and not be concerned about work. Writing this devotional has been a challenge as I have experienced many starts and stops. I self-imposed a deadline, which I missed, to get it to the publisher. Now, less than a week before I leave town for vacation, it, along with the other items on my agenda, must get done. Instead of allowing myself to get overwhelmed, I decided to have a little talk with Jesus.

When I asked the Good Spirit of God to lead me on a level path, the Holy Spirit helped me to prioritize my workload. With clarity and determination, I handle each day as it comes, completing what needs to be done for each day. When we operate in the will of God, there is no need to worry about tomorrow because tomorrow will worry about its own things (Matthew 6:34).

Instead, allow the Holy Spirit who dwells within us to guide us and lead us on a level path. If we are daily attuned and alert to the sound of the Holy Spirit, divine order will work through us. As we choose to live, move, and have our being in Christ, every step we take on our journey will be in the right direction. Seek God's will and allow the Lord's Good Spirit to lead you on a level path.

FAITH-ACTIVATING SONG

Listen to "Rain on Us" by Ernest Pugh
or "Just A Little Talk with Jesus"

PRAYER: Creator God, Teach and instruct me in the way that I should go. Provide counsel with Your eye on me. Allow the light of Jesus Christ to dispel darkness and reveal Your wisdom. May Your Good Spirit lead me on a level path. May Your guiding light shine on me and bless me with inspiration. I am grateful that the glory of the Lord resides within me guiding my every move. Amen.

REFLECTION:

Power and Strength

He gives power to the faint, and strengthens the powerless.
Isaiah 40:29

"How am I going to get it all done?" The answer is, I am not. When we try to operate in our own strength, we do not lean into the presence of the Lord. The Lord's name is strength and power. The Lord is a strong tower that makes us safe. There is nobody like the Lord. Without God, we cannot make it. Life is impossible without the Lord. Each morning when I rise, I call on the name of the Lord for help and guidance. The Amplified version of this verse reads, "He gives power to the faint and weary, and to him who has no might He increases strength [causing it to multiply and making it to abound]."

When I question how to get it all done, I trust God to increase His strength and power within me. When I have not had the best night's sleep, I seek to break the stronghold of yesterday so it will not kidnap today. I trust God to multiply His strength and make it abound, so I feel rested despite the limited number of hours that I slept. I can rise up and do what God is calling me to do in the moment. As I affirm God's power and strength in my life, I stand on God's Word so His power may abound.

FAITH-ACTIVATING SONG

Listen to "Nobody Greater" by VaShawn Mitchell

PRAYER: Lord, How excellent is Your name! Thank You for lifting me when I am faint. Thank You for Your strength and power which abides in me. Amen.

REFLECTION:

_____
_____
_____
_____
_____
_____
_____
_____
_____
_____
_____
_____
_____
_____
_____
_____
_____

Inner Strength

*I pray that, according to the riches of his glory,
he may grant that you may be strengthened in your inner being
with power through his Spirit.*
Ephesians 3:16

"Guess who is in our front yard?" asked my husband one Friday morning. "Our neighbor?" "No, it is our daughter." Biologically I have no children, but I married a widower who has two daughters, so I questioned more than stating the name of the youngest daughter. He responded no and said the name of the oldest daughter. Curiosity got the best of me, so I went to the window, and sure enough, she was outdoors putting up a Father's Day yard sign. My husband said, "You should say hello." My response was, "It is supposed to be a surprise. I am sure she thinks you are asleep and will not see this until later."

However, he persists on me saying hello as he sees this as an opportunity for his daughter and me to advance our relationship. I stand my ground because you cannot make something better that does not exist. My relationship, or lack thereof, with my adult daughters through marriage has been more challenging than I expected. Since they are adults with their own lives, I did not anticipate their resistance in establishing a relationship with me. I have learned not to take it personally. I realize it is not about me specifically but any woman who is a part of their dad's life.

I am prayerful as the journey continues, the love they have for their father will spill over and create a space in their heart to embrace me. In the meantime, I pray God will grant me strength in my inner-being to stay encouraged and keep the faith.

FAITH-ACTIVATING SONG

Listen to "We Are One Body" by Millennium Three

PRAYER: God, grant me the serenity to accept the things I cannot change, courage to change the things I can, and wisdom to know the difference. I release people and situations which are beyond my control into Your hands. Lord, I ask that You heal hearts and mend broken places of my loved ones. As You heal and mend, provide strength to their inner-being with power. Amen.

REFLECTION:

_____
_____
_____
_____
_____
_____
_____
_____
_____
_____
_____
_____
_____

Hope for My Soul

When I thought, "My foot is slipping," your steadfast love, O Lord, held me up. When the cares of my heart are many, your consolations cheer my soul.
Psalm 94:18-19

Consoling others is not my gift. I know death and sickness are not fun for anyone, but some people are better at offering words of comfort or practicing the ministry of presence. I never imagined I would become a pastor because one of the main characteristics is to provide comfort, and it is a challenge for me. While I struggle to provide solace, I sometimes seek consolation. During a difficult season in my life, I felt so alone. However, as I shared my predicament with others with the hopes of obtaining comfort, none came.

Instead of "consolation to cheer my soul," I heard "stop having a pity party." Whether I was having a pity party or not, I did not feel good. My foot was slipping, and when I tried to grab on with my hand, it was slipping too. But God's steadfast love held me up. The cares of my heart were heavy, but God's comfort and concern for me cheered my soul. When human help fails, trust God to give you hope that better days are coming.

FAITH-ACTIVATING SONG

Listen to "Better Days" by Ant Clemons with Kirk Franklin featuring Justin Timberlake

PRAYER: Lord God, Thank You for tender comfort and care. Thank You for holding me up and letting me know that better days are coming. As You comfort and encourage me, I will encourage others to keep their head up and their hope alive. Better days are coming so don't quit. Instead, activate Your faith. Amen.

REFLECTION:

_____
_____
_____
_____
_____
_____
_____
_____
_____
_____
_____
_____
_____
_____
_____
_____

Glory and Hope!

For what is our hope or joy or crown of boasting before our Lord Jesus at his coming? Is it not you? Yes, you are our glory and joy!
1 Thessalonians 2:19-20

"Yes, yes, yes!!!" I exclaimed with joy as I read the General Conference New Digest: Election Results and learned that one of the four newly elected Bishops of the African Methodist Episcopal church was a woman. I was pulling for her and praying for her. I was hopeful but not certain. In this male-dominated arena, I just was not certain. But God knew.

A few hours before the election, she posted Psalm 139 in her Facebook feed. I immediately pulled up my Bible app to read Psalm 139. Four verses were already highlighted; one being verse sixteen in the NRSV, "Your eyes beheld my unformed substance. In your book were written all the days that were formed for me when none of them as yet existed".

God knew for her, as well as the other newly elected Bishops, General Officers, and Judicial Council members, that this day was coming. Her campaign slogan was "opening doors for Jesus, jobs, and justice" because she knows Jesus is not only for her but for everybody. Jesus is our glory and joy, and He belongs to us all. Keep your hope up because glory is right around the corner. God is calling us to stay prepared and ready to serve until Jesus comes.

FAITH-ACTIVATING SONG

Listen to "It Belongs to Me" by Juan and Lisa Winans

PRAYER: Lord God, Thank You reshaping and shifting culture. While change appears slow, things are daily changing. Each day we are a little older and hopefully a little wiser. Thank You for moving the church universal to be open to move from what is, to what could be. I praise God that glory is just around the corner. I am prepared and ready to serve until Jesus comes. Amen.

REFLECTION:

Conquering Faith

For whatever is born of God conquers the world. And this is the victory that conquers the world, our faith.
1 John 5:4

My cellphone rings, and I look down to see my brother is calling. He is the primary caregiver of our parents, so my antenna goes up whenever he calls from North Carolina. I immediately answer the phone. Fortunately, it turns out, he just needs to share his experience for the day. As the "Uber driver" to various doctor appointments, he has a multitude of stories that can only be shared with family. After a couple of phone calls and some texts, we came up with some options to utilize if today's scenario arises again. There will be constant challenges with caregiving, but you cannot give up on your loved ones.

As children of God, the Lord does not give up on us, and as a result, we are not defeated. Our faith enables us to conquer the challenges that face us. Every day is not sunny, and every situation is not filled with joy, but we have victory in Jesus Christ, who has conquered the world. We are joint-heirs with Christ, so if you don't have a friend or family member to share your daily escapades with, the Lord always has a listening ear. Praise Him in advance as you move forward and claim the victory.

FAITH-ACTIVATING SONG

Listen to "Praise Him Advance" by Marvin Sapp

PRAYER: Lord God, Victory belongs to You. As we go about the day, remind us that we are more than conquerors in You. I praise You in advance for the victory. Amen.

REFLECTION:

Hope Filled

May the God of hope fill you with all joy and peace in believing, so that you may abound in hope by the power of the Holy Spirit.
Romans 15:13

Recently I took the Enneagram personality test. My primary personality type is a One, and in a nutshell, Ones are defined by their belief that everything must be in order and by their feeling that they must always be "right." At their core, Ones are the "model children" of the Enneagram world - dutiful, responsible, and perfection-seeking. In Biblical times the religious leaders felt they were always right as they tried to trip Jesus up. The Jewish people felt superior to the Gentiles.

However, Jesus was for everyone, and Paul, the author of Romans, taught the Gospel of Jesus Christ. Romans 15:13 comes at the end of a passage where he is sharing that the Gospel is for both Jews and Gentiles alike. It does not matter who we are, what we've done, or where we have been. The Good News is available if we choose to receive it. Regardless of our personality type or spiritual gifts, we all have value in Jesus Christ.

Just as your Enneagram results depict opportunities for development and growth, so our life in Christ depicts the fruit of the Spirit where the hope of God will fill you with joy and peace in believing so that you may abound in all hope with the power of the Holy Spirit. We are all a work-in-progress so keep your hope up as you pursue your dream anchored in the Lord.

FAITH-ACTIVATING SONG

Listen to Hymn "When Peace Live a River
(It Is Well with My Soul)

PRAYER: Lord God, I may not be where I want to be, but praise God I am not where I used to be. As I continue to strive to be more like your Son Jesus, I can say it is well with my soul. Amen.

REFLECTION:

_____
_____
_____
_____
_____
_____
_____
_____
_____
_____
_____
_____
_____
_____

Heirs By Grace

*So that, having been justified by his grace,
we might become heirs according to the hope of eternal life.*
Titus 3:7

"Do you want to be cremated?" We asked my dad. His consistent reply to this yes or no question was, "It does not matter to me; I will not be here." All I could do was shake my head. As our parents continue to age, questions about the end of life are more relevant. However, since our parents are not ready to discuss funeral arrangements or provide the location of the insurance information, all we can do is continue to ask questions and plant the seeds. While we hope to live as long as possible in the best health possible, we all know our time on earth is limited. We need to plan for our departure by preparing wills, establishing a power of attorney, and making decisions for the end of life.

Jesus did not need to establish a power of attorney because all power was in His hands. A lawyer was not required to execute His will or manage His estate because when He ascended into heaven to sit at the right hand of His Father, He sent us an Advocate to guide us. As children of God, we know that we are included, not because of anything we have done but because of God's sufficient grace. I am grateful for the grace of God that makes us heirs according to the hope of eternal life.

FAITH-ACTIVATING SONG

Listen to "God's Grace" by Rev. Luther Barnes and the Restoration Worship Center Choir

PRAYER: God, Thank You for Your saving grace that has kept me through all of these years. Please continue to guide and direct me so I may inherit the hope of eternal life. Amen.

REFLECTION:

Hope in the Lord

Those who hope in the LORD will renew their strength.
They will soar on wings like eagles; they will run and not grow weary,
they will walk and not be faint.
Isaiah 40:31 NIV

Isaiah 40:31 is one of my favorite scriptures. It probably is my favorite Old Testament verse, while Philippians 4:6-7 are my favorite verses in the New Testament. I do not remember when I latched on to Isaiah 40:31, but in my season of singleness, I was partial to translations that said, "those who wait." I encouraged myself to wait on the Lord. A friend of mine who has the gift of intercessory prayer prayed this verse for and with me at a women's retreat. As she proclaimed the scripture verbally, I danced the scripture physically. I knew I was not waiting idle but that God was preparing me for something that I could not handle right then.

Other translations of Isaiah 40:31 use "trust," and as I trusted the Lord and did not lean to my own understanding, He directed my path. When I began to get weary, the Lord renewed my strength to run on a little while longer. Now I have a new outlook for the future as a wife, a pastor, and the number of other roles God sees fit to place me in. God is Sovereign, and He can and will do what He wants when He wants, and how He wants. Place your hope in God and get ready to soar.

FAITH-ACTIVATING SONG

Listen to "Sovereign" by Daryl Coley

PRAYER: Jehovah Jireh, I praise You for renewing my strength when I am weak. I exalt Your name for giving the me the ability to mount up on wings like an eagle to complete the Kingdom work You are calling me to do. Lord, I'm running trying to make 100 because 99 1/2 will not do. So, thank You for allowing me to run in Your presence and in the embrace of Your rest so I do not get weary and not faint. Praise God, and Amen.

REFLECTION:

Speak Hope

Don't use foul or abusive language. Let everything you say be good and helpful, so that your words will be an encouragement to those who hear them.
Ephesians 4:29 NLT

The mouth and heart are connected. *"For whatever is in your heart determines what you say"* (Matt. 12:34, NLT). Change the heart, and you change the speech. Change the heart and speak life. Let everything you say be good and helpful. Now, if we think back, everything that has been said by us (or to us) has not been good or helpful. Why? Because we are not perfect people. Yet we are striving for perfection; every day, we are striving to be better than the day before.

So, fill the heart with the love of Christ so that only truth and honor can come out of the mouth. "Let your speech be always with grace, seasoned with salt" (Col. 4:6). Paul tells us to speak in such a way that what we say will build up our hearers and not tear them down. Draw others to Christ as your words minister grace and provide hope.

Speak life by declaring the Words of Luke 1:37 "For nothing will be impossible with God." That is a helpful Word to speak into your life and the lives of those you love. No matter what you are going through, no matter what you are facing, no matter what you have or have not accomplished at this point in your life, with God, you can still finish strong. As you trust God, speak out loud what's in your heart and your mouth. Encourage yourself and others to activate their faith by speaking hope.

FAITH-ACTIVATING SONG

Listen to "Take the Limits Off" by Israel Houghton & New Breed

PRAYER: Creator God, Thank You for giving me the strength to activate my faith and speak life over my situation and circumstance. As I speak life, may everything I say be good and helpful to those who hear, including myself. May everything I say bring hope and encouragement that nothing is impossible with You Lord. So, I take the limits off and launch into the deep to accomplish what is mine to do. Amen!

REFLECTION:

About the Author

Joy Wilkerson Yancy lives by Philippians 4:6 and truly believes in presenting everything to God with praise and thanksgiving. She is a witness that when you turn your situation over to God and leave it there, he will show up on time. When she surrendered to God's plans for her life, she was appointed as Pastor of Mt. Herman AME Church in Millington, TN. Shortly thereafter, she met her soon-to-be husband.

After fifty-plus years as a single lady, the Lord showed up mightily, and she married David Yancy II in the middle of a pandemic. As fellow pastors and preachers of the Gospel, they have come together as Yancy Ministries, where they equip and encourage not only their congregations but all those in their sphere of influence to let their light shine.

Joy lets her light shine and inspires others monthly on her "Final Friday Word" on Facebook Live on the last Friday of each month at 6:33 a.m. CST. She provides practical words of wisdom and encouragement to motivate her audience to keep their hope up and pursue God's purpose for their life.

A survivor of clinical depression, Joy is an expert on keeping your hope up and exercising your faith. During trials and mountains, she has continued to give God the praise for everything the Creator has brought her through. The author of several books and devotionals, this wife, pastor, preacher, sister, daughter, friend, author, and "Write by Faith" coach encourages you to keep your hope up as you give God praise. For more information, go to www.joywyancy.com.